Life in Numbers

What Is Average?

Lesley Ward

Publishing Credits

Rachelle Cracchiolo, M.S.Ed., *Publisher*
Conni Medina, M.A.Ed., *Managing Editor*
Nika Fabienke, Ed.D., *Series Developer*
June Kikuchi, *Content Director*
Susan Daddis, M.A.Ed., *Editor*
Kevin Pham, *Graphic Designer*

The TIME logo is a registered trademark of TIME Inc. Used under license.

Image Credits: p.8 Ruaridh Connellan/BarcroftImages/Barcroft Media via Getty Images; p.10 Claudio Zaccherini/Shutterstock; p.13 (top) James Ambler/Barcroft USA/Getty Images; p.13 Hackenberg-Photo-Cologne/Alamy; p.15 Courtesy of Carrie Swidecki; p.18 Kathy Hutchins/Shutterstock; p.20 (bottom), 21 Ruaridh Connellan/BarcroftImages/Barcroft Media via Getty Images; pp.26–27 Friedrich Stark/Alamy; pp.28–29 Lou Linwe/Alamy; p.33 (bottom) Zuma Press/Alamy; pp.34–35 Xinhua/Sipa USA/Newscom; p.35 Gary Gershoff/WireImage for PMK/HBH; pp.36–37 aperturesound/Shutterstock; p.38 kamui29/Shutterstock; p.39 nevenm/Shutterstock; pp.44–45 Shi Yali/Shutterstock; p.48 Vincenzo De Bernardo/Shutterstock; all other images from iStock and/or Shutterstock.

All companies and products mentioned in this book are registered trademarks of their respective owners or developers and are used in this book strictly for editorial purposes; no commercial claim to their use is made by the author or the publisher.

Library of Congress Cataloging-in-Publication Data

Names: Ward, Lesley, author.
Title: Life in numbers : what is average? / Lesley Ward.
Other titles: What is average?
Description: Huntington Beach, CA : Teacher Created Materials, [2018] | Audience: Grades 4 to 6. | Includes index.
Identifiers: LCCN 2017056310 (print) | LCCN 2018001488 (ebook) | ISBN 9781425854737 (e-book) | ISBN 9781425849979 (pbk.)
Subjects: LCSH: Average--Juvenile literature. | Mathematics--Juvenile literature. | Statistics--Juvenile literature.
Classification: LCC QA297 (ebook) | LCC QA297 .W347 2018 (print) | DDC 519.5/33--dc23
LC record available at https://lccn.loc.gov/2017056310

Teacher Created Materials

5301 Oceanus Drive
Huntington Beach, CA 92649-1030
www.tcmpub.com

ISBN 978-1-4258-4997-9
© 2019 Teacher Created Materials, Inc.

Table of Contents

What Is Average? 4
We the People 8
Fun and Games 14
Furry Friends 20
School Daze 26
Definitely *Not* Average! 35
Life of Averages 40
Glossary 42
Index 44
Check It Out! 46
Try It! 47
About the Author 48

What Is Average?

The word *average* can have different definitions. So, what exactly *is* an average? When you use math, an average, or mean, is a "balancing point" for a set of data. You calculate an average by adding numbers and dividing the total by how many numbers there are. The result is the average.

For example, to find the average of 4, 5, and 9, just add them up. The answer is 18. Now, divide 18 by 3, which is how many numbers you added. Easy—the answer is 6. So 6 is the average, or mean, of 4, 5, and 9.

Average can also mean not out of the ordinary. Many people equate average with boring, so they try not to be average or ordinary. They would rather be extraordinary and find difficult or unique things to make them stand out from the crowd.

Above-Average IQ

The average person has an intelligence quotient (IQ) of around 100. In 2016, Kashmea Wahi, an 11-year-old from England, scored 162 on an IQ test. That's two points higher than Albert Einstein! Wahi took the test because she figured that if she got a good score, her parents would know she was studying enough.

Batter Up!

Baseball players' batting averages are the number of hits divided by how many times they have been at bat. Pros today have a batting average of around .260. Ted Williams played for the Boston Red Sox for three years. In 1941, he had the highest batting average that season—an incredible .406! No one has hit above .400 for a season since.

Everyday Averages

Averages play a part in our daily lives. A farmer might check the average monthly rainfall so he or she knows exactly when to plant crops. An engaged couple might check weather records, too, so they can plan their **nuptials** when there's the least chance of rain.

Have you heard the saying "April showers bring May flowers"? On average, the rainiest month in the United States is not April. It's June!

Students are affected by averages when they take tests. Does your teacher tell you the average score the class got on a test? Your teacher added everyone's test scores and divided the total by the number of students in the class.

People use averages every day. Averages give the amount that is typical for a group of people or things. And they allow people to compare themselves to a group without looking at a whole set of data.

In the Lab

Replication is important in experiments. Scientists repeat experiments in the lab many times. Then, they add up the results and find the average. They do this to **verify** their results.

Top of the Class

A valedictorian is the student with the highest grade-point average (GPA) at the end of high school. He or she often gives a speech at graduation. A person's GPA is calculated first by adding the grade points a student has earned. Then, it is divided by the number of classes he or she has taken. Singer Alicia Keys was the valedictorian of her high school in New York City.

We the People

In 2016, Broc Brown, a 19-year-old from Michigan, was the tallest teenager in the world. He is currently 7 feet 8 inches tall (2 meters 20 centimeters). Brown has grown at a rate of 6 in. (15 cm) a year, and if this continues, he is on course to be the tallest man in the world. Life can be tough for Broc. He can barely squeeze into his mother's car, and his size-28 feet require **custom-made** shoes.

Brown's height is definitely *not* average. The average American man stands about 5 ft. 9.5 in. (1.5 m 24 cm) tall. Average height varies by country. The tallest men are in the Netherlands, where the average height is around 6 ft. (1.8 m). The shortest men, on average, are in Indonesia, at 5 ft. 2 in. (1.5 m 5 cm).

Brown poses for a picture with his cousin.

The average height for an American woman is 5 ft. 4 in. (1.5 m 10 cm). That may seem short, but it's not the tiniest. The average woman in Guatemala is 4 ft. 10 in. (1.2 m 25 cm).

Boys and girls can experience growth **spurts** at different times. It's important to remember that no two people are alike, and everyone grows at different rates.

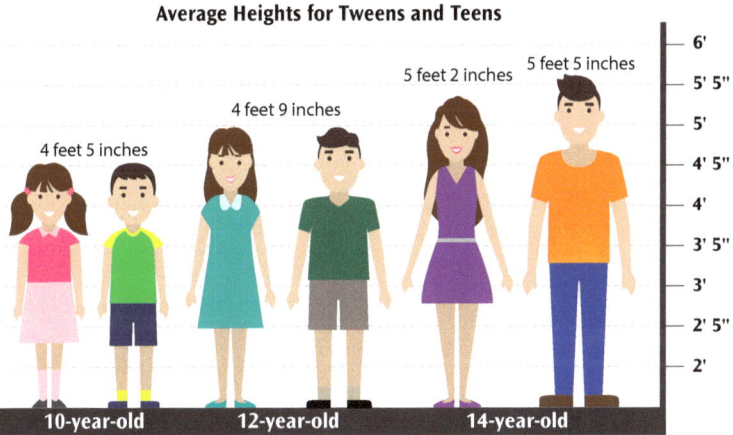

Average Heights for Tweens and Teens

- Grab a tape measure to see how tall you are. Are you above or below average?
- What trends do you notice about growth in teens from the chart?
- Do you eat a healthy diet, get enough sleep, and stay active? These things are **beneficial** to your growth and overall health.

Go Veggie!

Many people choose to become vegetarian or vegan for health reasons. People who eat a plant-based diet often have a lower risk of obesity, heart disease, and **diabetes**. Even if you don't choose to change your lifestyle, it's a good idea to skip a burger once in a while and grab a salad instead!

In China, people enjoy eating at their local restaurants.

Food for Thought

Diet varies from country to country. The foods people eat play a role in **longevity**. The average amount of food a person in the world eats is just over 4 pounds (1.8 kilograms) a day. Compare that with the average American, who eats 6 lb. (3 kg) a day.

In China, people eat about 5 lb. (2 kg) of food a day, but the **nutritional** value of their diet is drastically different from that of Americans. The average diets in China consist of about 3 percent sugars and fats each day. Compare that to the daily diets of Americans, which include 10 percent sugars and fats. The Chinese also eat about twice as much **produce** as Americans. On average, they **consume** almost 3 lb. (1.3 kg) of produce per day, while Americans eat just over 1.5 lb. (0.7 kg). Consuming fewer sugars and fats and eating more produce makes for a healthier diet.

We All Scream for Ice Cream

The average American eats almost 22 lb. (10 kg) of ice cream each year! Can you guess what the most popular flavor is? Believe it or not, it's vanilla, according to the International Ice Cream Association. What's your favorite flavor?

The Circle of Life

How long do people live? A recent study shows that the average **life expectancy** of an American man is 76 years. American women live about 5 years longer.

People on the Greek island of Ikaria live longer on average. They live about 10 years longer than Americans or Europeans. Scientists believe the cause of this is their diet, which includes a lot of vegetables and olive oil. The people there are also proponents of stress-free living. They take naps in the afternoons.

On the other end of the **spectrum** are places where the average life expectancy is short. Some countries are torn apart by wars. Sometimes, harsh weather conditions, such as droughts, affect life spans. In the African country of Chad, many people die of diseases, such as measles and malaria. Chad has the lowest life expectancy in the world—50 years.

Secrets to a Long Life

One of the oldest people to have ever lived was Jeanne Calment. She was born in 1875 in Arles, France. She outlived her husband, daughter, and grandson. The people in her town believed that eating chocolate, riding her bike, and using olive oil on her skin helped her live a long life. Calment rode her bike until she turned 100 and lived on her own until she was 110. She passed away in 1997 at the age of 122.

Table for 21, Please

A recent study revealed that American moms have an average of two children. But the Bates family of Tennessee didn't get that memo. Gil and Kelly Jo have 19 children, and the family has its own reality TV show.

Ikarian man hauls hay on his back.

Fun and Games

People love to have fun, and one of the most popular types of entertainment is gaming. The average American under the age of 13 spends a lot of time playing video games on a phone, a tablet, a computer, or a **console**. How much time? About two hours a day!

That's nothing compared to these people! Carrie Swidecki (swi-DEH-kee) of California holds the world record for the overall longest video-game marathon. She played *Just Dance* for 138 hours! Swidecki loves to boogie, but she's also **philanthropic** (fih-lehn-THRAH-pihk). Her real goal was to raise money for charity. She raised over $7,000 for children's hospitals for her efforts.

Joseph Kelly of England played *Minecraft* on his computer for more than 35 hours. He earned a place in the famous book, *Guinness World Records*.

Gaming isn't for everyone. Many people prefer other forms of entertainment. They go to the movies, watch TV, listen to music, and watch sports.

Glued to the TV

A study reported that the average 6- to 11-year-old spends 28 hours a week watching TV. The number of hours goes up if a child has a TV in his or her bedroom. These kids watch an average of almost 1.5 more hours per day.

A Day in the Life

A typical American teenager leads a busy life Monday through Friday. Between school and activities, there's not a lot of time for other things. Look at the circle graphs, and compare what teenage boys and girls do during a typical 24-hour school day.

Answer these questions using the graphs:

- Compare and contrast how boys and girls spend a typical day.
- What surprises you the most about these graphs?

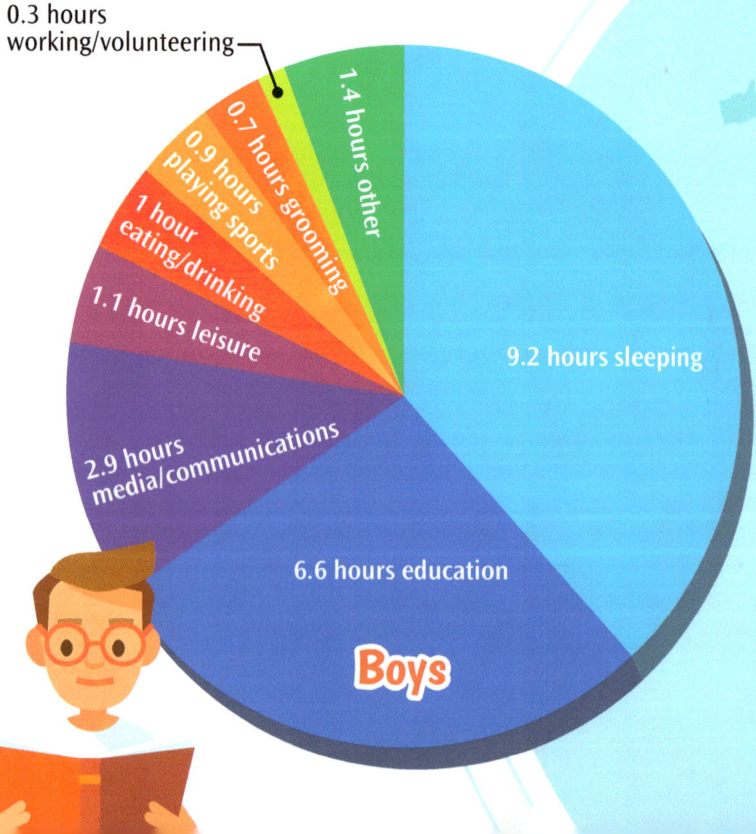

0.3 hours working/volunteering
0.7 hours grooming
0.9 hours playing sports
1 hour eating/drinking
1.1 hours leisure
1.4 hours other
2.9 hours media/communications
6.6 hours education
9.2 hours sleeping

Boys

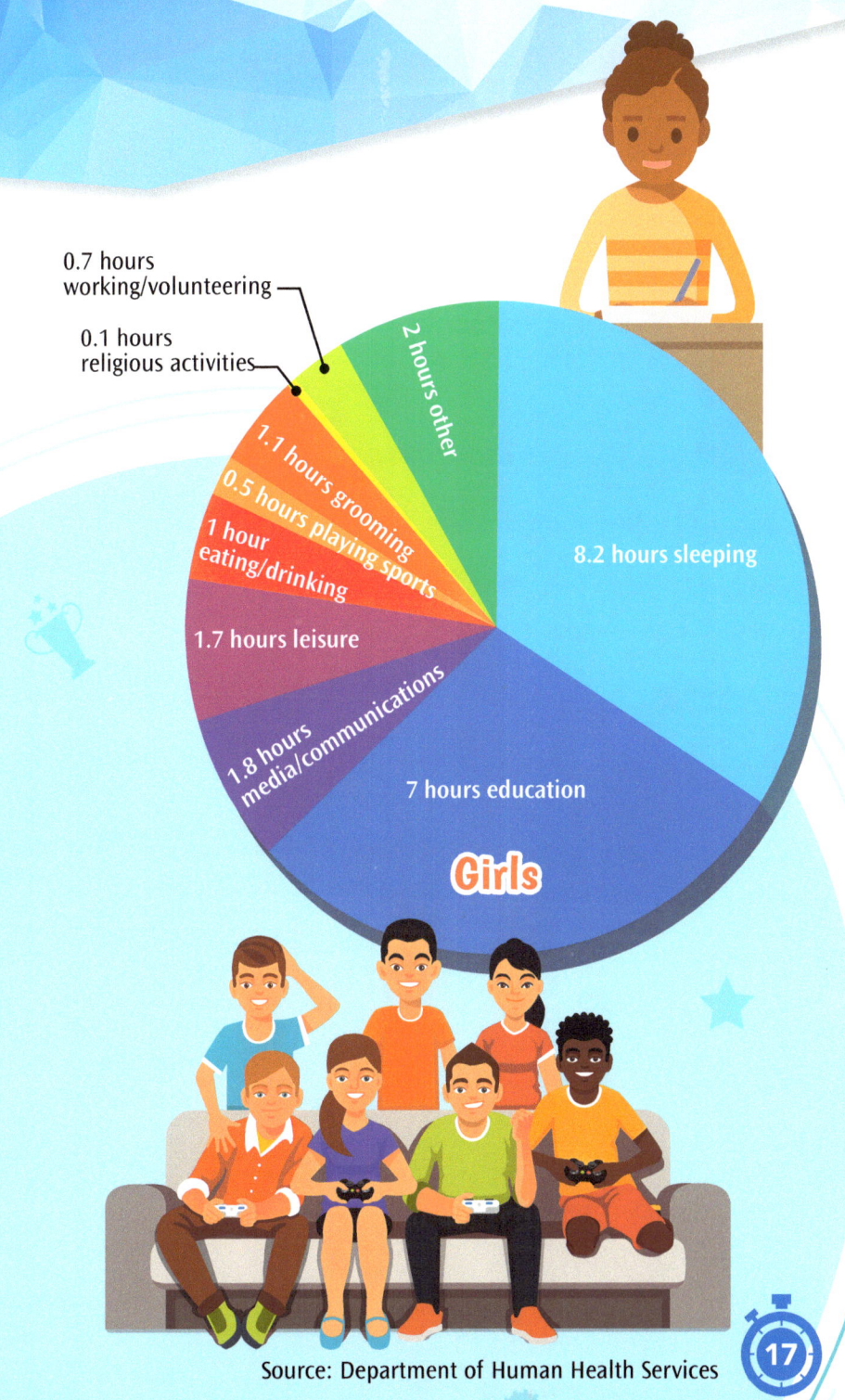

Source: Department of Human Health Services

Streaming Songs

Many teens and adults love music, and they wear earbuds for a large part of the day. A recent survey reported that the average American spends more than 25 hours a week listening to music on a smartphone. In 2016, people streamed more than 250 billion songs. Through streaming services, anyone can play music and make playlists of their favorite tunes.

When people take out their earbuds, they make time to go to concerts to see their favorite singers and bands. In 2016, Bruce Springsteen made more money than any other artist from ticket sales for his concert tour. His show brought in over $268 million. Megastar Beyoncé was just behind him in second place. Coldplay was third.

Drake's No. 1

"One Dance" by Drake featuring Wizkid and Kyla was the most-streamed song in 2016. It topped one billion streams on Spotify. The same year, "One Dance" also won the Teen Choice Award for Choice R&B/Hip-Hop Song.

Listen and Learn

Podcasts are like radio shows that are spread over several episodes. You download them from the Internet. If you're interested in a subject, such as history or sports, check a podcasting app to see if there is a podcast about it.

Furry Friends

Lynea Lattanzio (lih-NAY-uh luh-TAN-zee-oh) moved out of her five-bedroom house and into a trailer on her property. She moved so that there would be more room for cats in her home. How many? More than 1,000!

Lattanzio began taking in cats more than 25 years ago. Since then, she estimates that she has lived with about 28,000 cats. Many of them have been adopted, but some have stayed with her. She currently has more than 500 cats that need loving homes.

Lattanzio is a veterinary technician by trade. But she is proud of her **moniker** of "crazy cat lady"! She is also proud of her charity called Cat House on the Kings. There are no cages at Cat House, and no cat is **euthanized**.

Americans sure love furry felines. According to the American Veterinary Medical Association (AVMA), 30 percent of U.S. households have cats.

Colossal Cat

A typical male cat weighs 8–12 lb. (4–5 kg), but Samson is far from average! He is New York City's largest feline resident, weighing in at 28 lb. (13 kg) and measuring 4 ft. (1 m) long. Samson, a Maine Coon, is very popular. He has more than 150,000 followers on Instagram®.

Lattanzio stands in the kitchen of her home.

Tara to the Rescue!

In 2014, Jeremy Triantafilo (tree-AN-tah-FEE-loh) was playing in his front yard when a neighbor's dog ran up and bit him. The family cat, Tara, **interceded**. She attacked the dog. The attack was caught on a video, which went viral. Tara became known as the "hero cat."

The Most Popular Pet

There are almost 70 million dogs in the United States, making canines the top pet. A recent study by the AVMA says that almost 37 percent of U.S. households have at least one pup. Why are dogs so popular? According to doctors, there is a medical benefit to owning a dog. Petting a dog reduces stress and lowers blood pressure.

Sneaky Snuggler

In 2016, nine-year-old Josh Breaux of Louisiana sneaked into his neighbor's garage after school to give her dog a hug. He didn't know a security camera was taping him. The video went viral! Breaux's parents got him his own dog, a Labrador retriever named Drake.

Many people treat their dogs like children and show off pictures of their pets to friends and family. They get tattoos of their pooches. They even enter contests for people who look like their dogs! The average amount dog owners spend each year on their pet's vet care, food, treats, grooming, and toys is $1,641.

Small dogs tend to live longer than big dogs, but the average lifespan of most dogs is 10–13 years. Chihuahuas are one of the longest-living breeds, with an average lifespan of 15–17 years.

Pampered Pooches

Most dogs are **content** in an average doghouse, which can cost up to $300. One family in England went overboard when they built a **veritable** pooch palace for their two Great Danes. The house cost around $400,000! It has heated beds, a sound system, self-cleaning bowls, and a plasma TV.

Crazy about Critters

A lot of Americans love pets, according to a recent survey. About 68 percent of U.S. households, or 85 million families, own some kind of pet. And it's not just cats and dogs. There are plenty of other types of critters out there.

In terms of sheer numbers, fish top the list. There are almost 160 million fish in U.S. homes. Pet owners also take care of 20 million birds, 9 million reptiles, and 14 million small animals, such as mice, rats, and hamsters. Large animals are on the list, too. There are more than 7 million horses!

Keeping pets is costly. For example, a hamster might cost around $10, but the cage and toys cost about $100. Expenses, including food and bedding, will average about $260 a year. For a small bird like a **budgerigar**, the annual expense is about $185.

San Francisco's Therapy Pig

Traveling on an airplane can be stressful. That's why San Francisco International Airport "hired" LiLou, a therapy pig, in 2016. She isn't your average pig, though. She walks around the airport and helps travelers unwind while they wait for flights. LiLou wears different costumes and can do tricks, too.

Wild Animals as Pets

Some Americans keep **exotic** animals as pets. This can be problematic for the animals, their owners, and the surrounding communities. A 2010 documentary, *The Elephant in the Living Room*, looks at the dark side of owning exotic animals. It's the story of two men whose lives collide. One is a police officer and animal **advocate**. The other is the owner of two lions. They meet when one of the lions escapes.

School Daze

Students from a small town in Colombia had an **unconventional** way to get to school. They used rope to attach themselves to a rusty zip line about 1,300 ft. (396 m) above the roaring Rio Negro. Then, they hurled themselves from a cliff and traveled at speeds up to 60 miles per hour (96 kilometers per hour) to the opposite bank. The students on the zip line traveled faster than the average city speed limit in Colombia, which is 40 mph (64 kmph) per hour! These students took this scary journey five days a week. Their school was located on the other side of the river, and this was the only way to get there!

In India, students crowd into a *tuktuk*, a tiny truck with three wheels, to get to school. Riding a tuktuk is noisy and bumpy. But these students are determined to get to school. Their morning commute makes rides on buses or in your parents' cars seem pretty tame.

Bus Safety

Riding a public school bus is one way students get to school in the United States. There are 450,000 public school buses on the road every year. They transport over 23 million students to school and school-related events. Studies show that students who ride the bus are seven times safer than students who are driven to school by car or small truck.

Instead of making a three-hour walk to the other side of the river, this young man uses the zip line.

Riding in Style

In the past, most schoolkids in the United States rode the big yellow bus, but today the number one mode of transportation to and from school is the car. Riding the school bus comes second, and walking is third. Very few kids ride their bikes to school, and even fewer take public transportation, such as trains.

Hitting the Books

Have you ever calculated how many hours you spend at school each day? In the United States, the average school day is about 6.5 hours.

Students in other countries spend a lot more time in school. In some schools in China, classes begin at 7:30 a.m. and the last bell rings at 5:30 p.m. That is a 10-hour school day.

Chinese students have more studying to do when they get home. On average, they spend about 3 hours each night on homework. American students average about 6 hours of homework a week, which is just over an hour every day. The next time you want to complain about your homework, think about your Chinese **counterparts**!

Lifting Weights

Researchers in New York City weighed the backpacks of 50 students. The average backpack of sixth graders weighed 18.4 lb. (8 kg), while the heaviest one was 30 lb. (14 kg)! Doctors recommend that kids carry no more than one-fifth of their body weight, or they may hurt their backs.

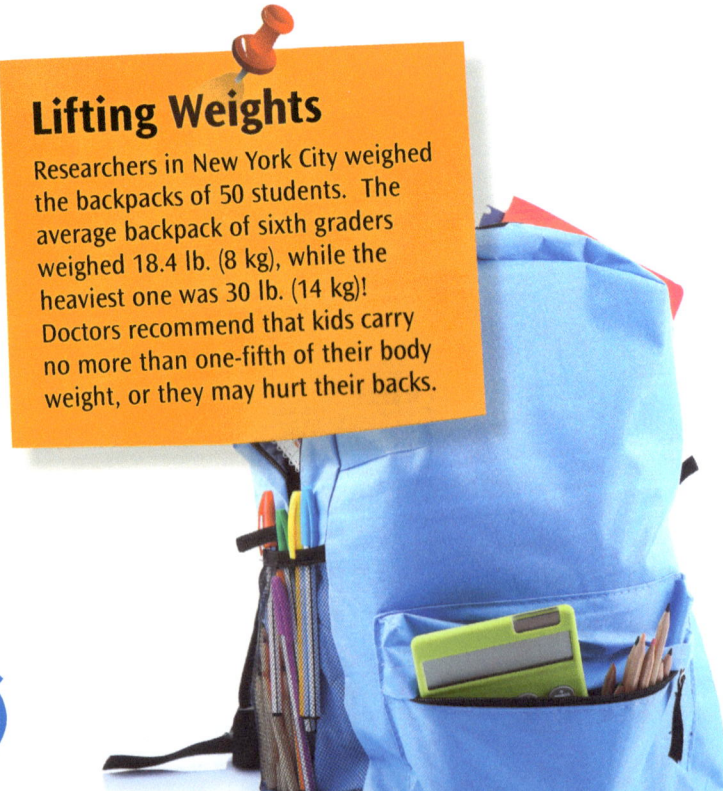

Chinese middle school students listen during a lesson.

Lunch Break

School isn't all work. Most students look forward to lunchtime, when they can hang out with their friends. But this social time is actually quite short. On average, students spend about 15–20 minutes in the cafeteria.

Is cafeteria food good or bad? Researchers recently compared school meals to bag lunches to see which are healthier. Turns out that the lunches from home were worse. They were higher in fat and sugar and lower in protein and calcium.

This means that cafeteria food is the more nutritious option for kids who need energy for after-school sports. Playing a sport, whether it's intramurals or for a team, is good for you because doctors recommend that kids exercise about 60 minutes a day.

History of School Lunches

Up until about the late 1900s, lunch was the largest meal of the day for many Americans. Workers and students went home to eat as a family. At the start of the 20th century, some groups became concerned about children not getting enough food. Philadelphia and Boston were the first two cities to begin school-lunch programs.

World Lunch

School lunches are different around the world. American students nibble on chicken nuggets, pizza, and even fast food from restaurants. Students in South Korea eat fish soup, tofu over rice, and fresh vegetables. In Kenya, schools offer *githeri*, a dish made of beans and dried corn.

typical American school lunch

Time to Quit

An ESPN poll asked kids why they quit a sport, and the top answer was, "I was not having fun!" The second reason for quitting was different for boys and girls. Girls said they wanted to concentrate more on studying, while boys said they had a health problem or an injury.

Sporty Students

In a recent study, football was chosen as the most popular high school sport in the United States, followed by track and field, then basketball. The study also showed that more students are trying uncommon sports, such as archery and badminton.

Playing a sport may take up a lot of time, but it may improve grades and your health. Athletes in middle school had an average GPA of 3.1, while non-athletes averaged 2.4. Participating in sports reduces the risk of being overweight or getting diabetes. Student athletes are also less likely to drop out of school. And they are more likely to go to college. If you don't play a sport, maybe it's time to join a team!

Sam's a Star

Sam Gordon has been playing football since she was nine. Thanks to her athletic skills and a video her dad posted on YouTube, Sam is famous. By the time the star running back was 10, she had appeared in an NFL video and on a Wheaties cereal box.

Giant Pizza Pie

The average size of a large pizza is 16 in. (40.6 cm), but some people in California thought that was far too small. In 2017, these people joined forces and created the longest pizza ever. It measured 1.3 mi. (2 km) long. Once the record was verified, everyone could take a slice.

Definitely *Not* Average!

Many people want to prove that they are not average. They are willing to do strange things to get attention. They hope that videos of them will go viral and make them celebrities.

Some people aspire to be included in the famous *Guinness World Records*. The book was first published in 1955. It was the **brainchild** of Sir Hugh Beaver, the chairman of Guinness Brewery in Ireland. He wanted a book of facts and figures that people could read if they had a question about something. The book is published every year and is full of new facts and many wacky world records. The people who appear in *Guinness World Records* are far from average!

Nail Tale

The record for the longest fingernails on a pair of female hands belongs to Lee Redmond of Utah. She didn't cut her nails for 30 years, and they each measured almost 3 ft. (1 m) long. Redmond broke her nails in a car accident in 2009, and she never grew them long again.

Be a Record Breaker

Anybody can apply to be in the *Guinness World Records*. It doesn't matter how old you are, what language you speak, or where you live. You don't have to be an Olympic athlete or a rocket scientist either.

First, study the *Guinness World Records* book and website because most people who are featured break existing records. Then, decide which record you want to attempt to break. The book's guidelines state that if something can't be weighed, measured, or counted, it's probably not a record.

There are hundreds of records listed in the *Guinness World Records* book. You can **perfect** your skills at home. For example, practice eating M&Ms® with chopsticks for 60 seconds while wearing a blindfold. The record is 20! Or chew some gum and blow the biggest bubble! To break the record, your bubble must be bigger than 20 in. (50.8 cm).

More than 50,000 people apply each year to get into the *Guinness World Records*.

> Why do you think so many people try to set new world records?

> Would you like to be in the *Guinness World Records*? For what? Explain why.

Lucky's Tattoos

A recent survey found that 3 out of 10 U.S. adults have one or more tattoos. But the most tattooed man in the world has them beat. Lucky Diamond Rich has his entire body tattooed. When he's not in the tattoo parlor, Rich spends his time juggling chain saws, swallowing swords, and riding his unicycle!

Before trying to break a record, read all of the rules. *Guinness World Records* is serious about safety, so do not try anything that puts you or others in danger.

To be considered, you must first fill out an application. If the people at *Guinness World Records* approve it, then an **adjudicator** may travel to you. He or she must verify that you have actually broken a record. You can also show proof of your **feat** by sending in a video, photos, and two witness statements.

If your record is accepted, you will receive a certificate and appear in the book and on the website. And you'll have bragging rights for the rest of your life!

Pokémon Obsession!

Lisa Courtney of the United Kingdom owns the largest collection of Pokémon **memorabilia**. She has traveled to Japan several times to collect merchandise. She now owns more than 17,000 items!

Plenty of Piercings

Elaine Davidson is the world's most pierced woman. She won the title in 2000 with over 400 piercings. By 2011, she had almost 7,000! There are 192 on her face.

Life of Averages

Now that you know about averages, try to figure out some averages in your daily life. How long do you typically wait in line in the cafeteria? Time yourself every day for a week, and then figure out the average. Do you remember how to do that? Add up the time spent in line and then divide it by the number of days in the week. Then, you'll know how much time on average you spend waiting for cafeteria food!

If your parents get a really big water bill, they might want to know the average time you spend in the shower every day. You can also calculate the average number of hours of sleep you get at night and see if it **correlates** with how well you do in school. Averages affect everyone. They might not always be exciting, but they are important!

The Law of Averages

The so-called "Law of Averages" is a myth. It is the false belief that if an experiment is performed a few times, the result will balance itself out. For example, you flip a coin, and the result is heads five times in a row. The Law of Averages leads people to believe that the next five flips will be tails. But each flip has an equal chance of being heads or tails.

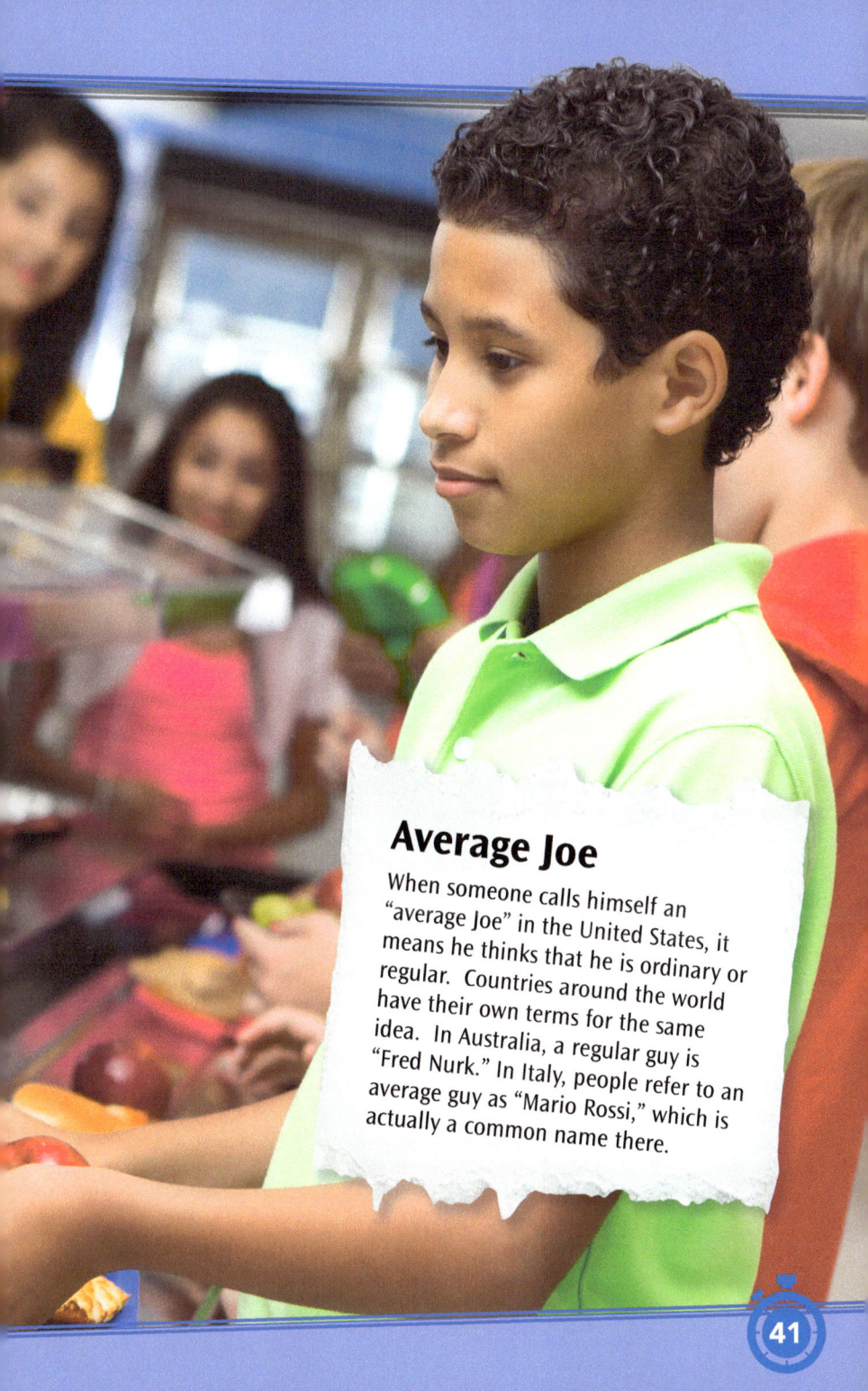

Average Joe

When someone calls himself an "average Joe" in the United States, it means he thinks that he is ordinary or regular. Countries around the world have their own terms for the same idea. In Australia, a regular guy is "Fred Nurk." In Italy, people refer to an average guy as "Mario Rossi," which is actually a common name there.

Glossary

adjudicator—a person who judges a competition

advocate—a person who publicly supports a cause

beneficial—producing something that is good for you

brainchild—an idea someone came up with

budgerigar—a small yellow and green parrot, usually kept as a pet; often called a parakeet

console—a system that hooks up to a display to play video games

consume—to eat or drink

content—happy, satisfied

correlates—shows a close relationship

counterparts—people or things that resemble or act like each other

custom-made—specially made to meet the needs of a specific person

diabetes—a disease in which a person's blood sugar levels are too high, resulting in other health problems

euthanized—put to death

exotic—foreign; from another area of the world

feat—great accomplishment

interceded—settled an argument or fight

life expectancy—how long something lasts or someone lives, especially based on a norm or average

longevity—the length of one's life

memorabilia—objects collected or kept because of historical interest

moniker—nickname

nuptials—wedding

nutritional—relating to healthy foods

perfect—to make something better or perfect

philanthropic—generous; giving

produce—fresh fruits and vegetables

replication—a copy of something

spectrum—a range of data

spurts—sudden increases in activity

unconventional—not the usual way of doing things

verify—make sure that something is true or accurate

veritable—prove true

Index

backpacks, 28
Bates, Gil and Kelly Jo, 13
Beaver, Sir Hugh, 35
Beyoncé, 18
Boston Red Sox, 5
Breaux, Josh, 22
Brown, Broc, 8
cats, 20–21, 24
Cat House on the Kings, 20
China, 10–11, 28–29
Coldplay, 18
Courtney, Lisa, 38
Davidson, Elaine, 39
dog, 21–24
Drake (dog), 22
Drake (singer), 18
Gordon, Sam, 33
grade point average (GPA), 7, 33
Guinness World Records, 14, 35–36, 38

Ikaria, Greece, 12–13
intelligence quotient (IQ), 4
Just Dance, 14
Kelly, Joseph, 14
Keys, Alicia, 7
Lattanzio, Lynea, 20–21
Law of Averages, 40
LiLou (pig), 24
Minecraft, 14
Pokémon, 38
Redmond, Lee, 35
Rich, Lucky Diamond, 37
Samson (cat), 20
Springsteen, Bruce, 18
Swidecki, Carrie, 14–15
Tara (cat), 21
Triantafilo, Jeremy, 21
Wahi, Kashmea, 4
Williams, Ted, 5
YouTube, 33

Check It Out!

Books

Boyer, Crispin. 2015. *National Geographic Kids Why? Over 1,111 Answers to Everything.* Washington, DC: National Geographic.

Ghigna, Charles. 2016. *Strange, Unusual, Gross & Cool Animals (An Animal Planet Book).* New York: Liberty Street.

Schwartz, Gary. 2015. *The King of Average.* North Bend, WA: Bunny Moon Enterprise, LLC.

TIME FOR KIDS. 2011. *Big Book of Science Experiments.* New York: TIME FOR KIDS Books.

Videos

Dunham, Duwayne, dir. 1994. *Little Giants.* Warner Bros.

Freudenthal, Thor, dir. 2010. *Diary of a Wimpy Kid.* 20th Century Fox.

Websites

Cat House on the Kings. www.cathouseonthekings.com.

Guinness Book of World Records. www.guinnessworldrecords.com.

Math Playground. www.mathplayground.com.

Sports Illustrated Kids. www.sikids.com.

Try It!

You can figure out some averages in your daily life. You will need a notebook to write down and organize your findings and a calculator to figure out the averages.

- For one week, track how you spend your time. This can include eating, sleeping, school, sports, screen time, and more.

- Write down the minutes and hours in your journal.

- At the end of the week, figure out your averages. Add the numbers and then divide them by seven.

- Compare your averages with the averages in this book or with friends. Present your findings using visuals.

About the Author

Lesley Ward is an author and a former children's magazine editor. Now, she lives on a farm in the heart of the Kentucky Bluegrass. She shares her farm with 3 horses and 2 dogs. The average household number of cats in the United States is 2.1, but Ward exceeds that. She is the proud owner of 7 friendly felines!